SACRED READING

for Lent 2016

SACRED READING

for Lent 2016

Apostleship of Prayer

Douglas Leonard, Executive Director

AVE MARIA PRESS AVE Notre Dame, Indiana

© 2015 by the Apostleship of Prayer

All rights reserved. No part of this book may be used or reproduced in any manner whatsoever, except in the case of reprints in the context of reviews, without written permission from Ave Maria Press®, Inc., P.O. Box 428, Notre Dame, IN 46556, 1-800-282-1865.

Founded in 1865, Ave Maria Press is a ministry of the United States Province of Holy Cross.

www.avemariapress.com

Paperback: ISBN-13 978-1-59471-611-9

E-book: ISBN-13 978-1-59471-612-6

Cover image © Thinkstock.

Cover and text design by David Scholtes.

Printed and bound in the United States of America.

CONTENTS

INTRODUCTION

In the Gospel, Jesus says his disciples will fast when he, the bridegroom, is taken from them. We know that Jesus is always with us, but during the season of Lent we honor him in a special way by entering a forty-day period of prayer, fasting, and almsgiving in preparation for the celebration of the resurrection of the Lord, Easter Sunday. The season of Lent begins on Ash Wednesday, dividing the cycle of Ordinary Time in the Church year. Sundays in Lent are not counted as fast days. Fast days continue through Holy Saturday, the day before Easter. Lent officially ends on Holy Thursday, the beginning of the Easter triduum.

The number of days of Lent corresponds to the forty days Jesus prayed and fasted in the desert before beginning his earthly ministry. Lent is a time to allow God to help us become holy, to help us look to the needs of others and minister to those needs, and most of all, to grow in faith, hope, and love, for those virtues are of God, motivating and empowering us to live the Gospel.

One of the important ways Christians observe Lent is by taking up—or practicing with greater intentionality—certain devotional or prayer practices to help them prepare to celebrate the Easter feast with greater joy. Christians throughout the world are rediscovering a powerful, ancient form of prayer known as "sacred reading" (lectio divina). What better way to deepen one's friendship with Jesus Christ, the Word of God, than by prayerfully encountering him in the daily Gospel?

Sacred reading is a spiritual practice guided by the Holy Spirit as you interact with the words of the daily Gospel. Those who engage the Gospels in this manner often find that the Lord speaks to them in intimate and surprising ways. They open their hearts to Jesus, and he opens his heart to them.

Saint Paul prays beautifully for his readers:

> For this reason I bow my knees before the Father, from whom every family in heaven and on earth takes its name. I pray that, according to the riches of his glory, he may grant that you may be strengthened in your inner being with power through his Spirit, and that Christ may dwell in your hearts through faith, as you are being rooted and grounded in love. I pray that you may have the power to comprehend, with all the saints, what is the breadth and length and height and depth, and to know the love of Christ that surpasses knowledge, so that you may be filled with all the fullness of God. (Eph 3:14–19)

How to Use This Book

This book will set you on a personal prayer journey with Jesus from Ash Wednesday through the end of Holy Week. *Please note that some of the readings in this booklet have been shortened for group use.* In each case the citation for the unabridged reading is marked with an asterisk (*), followed by a parenthetical citation that includes the verses in the booklet. *Sacred Reading: The 2016 Guide to Daily Prayer* contains the unabridged Gospel texts for the entire liturgical year and is available online through the Apostleship of Prayer website or through your local bookstore.

In prayerful reading of the daily Gospels, you join your prayers with those of believers all over the world. Following the readings for each season of the liturgical calendar, you will be invited each day to reflect on the Gospel text for the day in six simple but profound steps:

1. Know that God is present with you and ready to converse.

At all times God is everywhere, including where you are in this very moment. The human mind is incapable of fully grasping the mystery of God, but we do know some things about God from scripture. God is the transcendent ground of all being, invisible, eternal, and infinite in power. God is Love, with infinite love for you and me. God is one with and revealed through the Word, Jesus Christ, who became flesh. Through him all things were made, and by him and for him all things subsist. Jesus is the Way, the Truth, and the Life. He says that those who know him also know his Father. Through the passion, death, and resurrection of Jesus, we are reconciled with God. If we believe in Jesus Christ, we become the sons and daughters of Almighty God.

God gives us the Holy Spirit to lead us to truth and understanding. The Holy Spirit also gives us power to live obedient to the teachings of Jesus. The Holy Spirit draws us to prayer and works in us as we pray. No wonder we come into God's presence with gladness. All God's ways are good and beautiful. We can get to know God better by encountering God in the Word, which is Jesus himself.

The prompt prayer at the beginning of each day's reading is just that: a prompt, something to get you started. In fact, all the elements in the process of sacred reading are meant to prompt you to your own conversations with God. After reading the prompt, feel free to continue to pray in your own words: respond in your own way, pray in your own way, and hear God speaking to you personally. Your goal is to make sacred reading your own prayer time each day.

2. Read the Gospel.

The entire Bible is the Word of God, but the Gospels (Matthew, Mark, Luke, and John) specifically tell the Good News about Jesus Christ. Throughout the Church year, the daily Gospel readings during Mass will come from all four gospels. The Sacred Reading series (the prayer books as well as the seasonal booklets for Advent/Christmas and Lent/Easter) concentrates on praying with the daily Gospels. These readings contain the story of Jesus' life, his teachings, his works, his passion and death on the cross, his resurrection on the third day, and his ascension into heaven.

The Gospels interpret Jesus' ministry for us. Much more, by the Holy Spirit, we can find in the Gospels the very person of Jesus Christ. Prayerful reading of the daily Gospel is an opportunity to draw close to the Lord: Father, Son, and Holy Spirit. As we pray with the Gospels, we can be transformed by the grace of God—enlightened, strengthened, and moved. Seek to read the Gospel with a complete openness to what God is saying to you. Many who pray with the Gospel recommend rereading it several times.

3. *Notice what you think and feel as you read the Gospel.*

Sacred reading can involve every faculty—mind, heart, emotions, soul, spirit, sensations, imagination, and much more—though usually not all at once. Different passages touch different keys in us. Sometimes we may laugh. Sometimes we may need to stop and worship before we continue. Sometimes we will be puzzled, amazed, stung, abashed, reminded of something lovely, or reminded of something we had wanted to forget.

Seek to feel all of your emotions as you read. Apply your intellect, too. You will confront problems of context and exegesis on a daily basis. That's okay.

Sometimes you may experience very little. That's okay, too. God is at work anyway. Give yourself to the Gospel and take from it what is there for you each day.

Most important, notice what in particular jumps out at you, whatever it may be. It may be a word, a phrase, a character, an image, a pattern, an emotion, a sensation—some arrow to your heart. Whatever it is, pay attention to it because the Holy Spirit is using it to accomplish something in you.

Sometimes a particular Gospel repeats during the liturgical year of the Church. To pray through the same Gospel even on successive days presents no problem whatsoever to your sacred reading. Saint Ignatius of Loyola, founder of the Jesuits and author of *The Spiritual Exercises*, actually recommends repeated meditation on passages of scripture. Read in the Spirit, Gospel passages have unlimited potential to reveal to us the truths we are ready to receive. For the receptive soul, the Word of God has boundless power to illuminate and transform the prayerful believer.

4. *Pray as you are led for yourself and others.*

Praying is just talking with God. Believe God hears you. Believe God will answer you. Believe God knows what you need even before you ask. Jesus says so in the Gospel. So your conversation with God can go far beyond asking for things. You may thank, praise, worship, rejoice, mourn, explain, question, reveal your fears, seek understanding, or ask forgiveness. Your conversation with God has no limits. God is the ideal conversationalist. God wants to spend much time with you.

Being human, we can't help being self-absorbed, but praying is not just about our own needs. We are often moved by the Gospel to pray for others. We will regularly remember our loved ones in prayer. Sometimes we will be led to pray for someone who has hurt us. At other times we will be moved to pray for a class of people in need, wherever they are in the world, such as for persecuted Christians, refugees, the mentally ill, teachers, the unborn, or the lonely.

We may also pray with the universal Church by praying for the pope's prayer intentions. Those intentions are entrusted to the Apostleship of Prayer and are available through its website and its annual and monthly leaflets. You may get your own copy of this year's papal prayer intentions by contacting the Apostleship of Prayer. The Apostleship is the pope's prayer group, with more than fifty million members worldwide. Jesus asked us to unite in prayer, promising that the Father would grant us whatever we ask for in his name.

5. *Listen to Jesus.*

Jesus the Good Shepherd speaks to his own sheep, who hear his voice (see Jn 10:27). This listening is a most wonderful time in your *Sacred Reading* prayer experience. The italicized words in this passage are the words I felt impressed upon my heart as I prayed with these readings. I included them in order to help you to listen more actively for whatever it is the Lord might be saying to you.

Jesus speaks to all in the Gospels, but in *Sacred Reading* he can now speak exclusively to you. If you can, write down what he says to you and reread his words during the day. Put all of Jesus' words to you in a folder or keep a spiritual notebook. Believers through the ages have recorded the words of Jesus to them, holy mystics and ordinary believers alike.

It takes faith to hear the voice of Jesus. This faith will grow as you practice listening. Ideally, we will learn to hear what Jesus is saying to us all day long, such as when we face difficult situations. Listening to the voice of Jesus is practicing the presence of God. As Saint Paul said, "In him we live and move and have our being" (Acts 17:28).

Saint Ignatius of Loyola called this conversation with Jesus *colloquy*. That word simply means that two or more people are talking. Saint Ignatius even urges us to include the saints in our prayer conversations. We believe in the communion of saints. If you have a patron saint, don't be afraid to talk to him or her. In her autobiography, Saint Thérèse of Lisieux, who was a member of the Apostleship of Prayer, describes how she spoke often with Mary and Joseph, as well as with Jesus.

6. *Ask God to show you how to live today.*

Pope Benedict XVI commented that sacred reading is not complete without a call to action: something in our praying leads us to do something in our day. Perhaps we find an opportunity to serve, to love, to give, to lead, or to do something good for someone else. Perhaps we find occasion to repent, to forgive, to ask forgiveness, to make amends. Open your heart to anything God might want you to do. Try to keep the conversation with God going all day long.

Asking God to show you how to live is the last step of the *Sacred Reading* prayer time, but that doesn't mean you need to end it here. Keep it going. You may drift off in the presence of God, lose attention, or even fall asleep, but you can come back. God is always present, seeking to love you and to be loved. God is always seeking to lead us to the green pastures. God is our strength, our rock, our ever-present help in time of trouble. God is full of mercy, ready to forgive us again and again. God sees us through very difficult times. God heals us. God gives his life to us constantly. God is our Maker, Father, Mother, Lover, Servant, Savior, and Friend. We know that from the Gospel. He is an inexhaustible spring of blessing and holiness in our innermost selves. The sanctification of our souls is God's work, not our own.

As you read, ask the Holy Spirit to lead you in this process. With genuine faith, open yourself to respond to the Word and the Spirit, and your relationship with

Jesus will continue to deepen and to grow just as the infant Jesus grew within the womb of the Blessed Mother. This in turn will lead you to share the love of Christ with all those you encounter—just as the Blessed Mother draws all those who encounter her directly to her Son.

Other Resources to Help You

These *Sacred Reading* resources, including both the seasonal books and the annual prayer book, are enriched by the spirituality of the Apostleship of Prayer. Since 1844 our mission has been to encourage Catholics to pray each day for the good of the world, the Church, and the prayer intentions of the Holy Father. In particular, we encourage Christians to respond to the loving gift of Jesus Christ by making a daily offering of themselves each day. As we give the Lord our hearts, we ask him to make them like his own Heart, full of love, mercy, and peace.

These booklets may be used in small groups or as a handy individual resource for those who want a special way to draw close to Christ during Lent. If you enjoy these reflections and would like to continue this prayerful reading throughout the year, pick up a copy of the *Sacred Reading* annual prayer guide. You can order one through the Apostleship of Prayer website or through avemariapress.com.

These annual books offer a personal prayer experience that can be adapted to meet your particular needs. For example, some choose to continue to reflect upon each day's reading in writing, either in the book or in a separate journal or notebook, to create a record of their spiritual journey for the entire year. Others supplement their daily reading from the book with the daily videos and other online resources available through the Apostleship of Prayer website (apostleshipofprayer.org).

For more information about the Apostleship of Prayer and about the other resources we have developed to help men and women cultivate habits of daily prayer, visit our website at apostleshipofprayer.org.

I pray that this experience may help you walk closely with God every day.

> Douglas Leonard, PhD
> Executive Director
> Apostleship of Prayer

We Need Your Feedback!
Ave Maria Press and the Apostleship of Prayer would like to hear from you. After you've finished reading, please go to **avemariapress.com/feedback** to take a brief survey about your experience with *Sacred Reading for Lent 2016*. We'll use your input to make next year's book even better.

WEEK OF ASH WEDNESDAY

In the face of so many wounds that hurt us and could lead to a hardness of heart, we are called to dive into a sea of prayer, which is the sea of the boundless love of God, in order to experience his tenderness.

Pope Francis
Ash Wednesday Mass
March 5, 2014

Wednesday, February 10, 2016
Ash Wednesday

Know that God is present with you and ready to converse.

As we begin this holy season of Lent, we offer ourselves to God, aware that we are sinners and dust that will return to the earth after our brief journey here. But the Lord will quicken us by the Spirit, and we shall live in him. How can we begin that new life now? "Father, you see me in secret. You are with me now. Let your Word speak life to me."

Read the Gospel: Matthew 6:1–6, 16–18.

Jesus said, "Beware of practicing your piety before others in order to be seen by them; for then you have no reward from your Father in heaven.

"So whenever you give alms, do not sound a trumpet before you, as the hypocrites do in the synagogues and in the streets, so that they may be praised by others. Truly I tell you, they have received their reward. But when you give alms, do not let your left hand know what your right hand is doing, so that your alms may be done in secret; and your Father who sees in secret will reward you.

"And whenever you pray, do not be like the hypocrites; for they love to stand and pray in the synagogues and at the street corners, so that they may be seen by others. Truly I tell you, they have received their reward. But whenever you pray, go into your room and shut the door and pray to your Father who is in secret; and your Father who sees in secret will reward you. . . .

"And whenever you fast, do not look dismal, like the hypocrites, for they disfigure their faces so as to show others that they are fasting. Truly I tell you, they have received their reward. But when you fast, put oil on your head and wash your face, so that your fasting may be seen not by others but by your Father who is in secret; and your Father who sees in secret will reward you."

Notice what you think and feel as you read the Gospel.

God is not impressed by grand gestures of piety done to impress others. When we do good, we should not gloat in our righteousness. What does this Gospel say about almsgiving, praying, and fasting?

Pray as you are led for yourself and others.

"Father, you want me to have a secret friendship with you. Help me to love and serve you for your own sake, not for appearance's sake . . ." (Continue in your own words.)

Listen to Jesus.

You are beginning the season of Lent, preparing yourself for the Church's commemoration of my passion, crucifixion, and

*resurrection. How may I help you make this Lent especially
meaningful?* What else is Jesus saying to you?

Ask God to show you how to live today.

Linger in the presence of Jesus as he offers himself
to you again by his Word and his Spirit. Respond to
his love for you. "Jesus, you are generous with me.
Show me how to be generous with others today. I offer
myself and all I am and have to you. Amen."

Thursday, February 11, 2016

**Know that God is present with
you and ready to converse.**

"I am following you, Jesus, in your passion and in your
triumphant resurrection."

Read the Gospel: Luke 9:22–25.

Jesus said, "The Son of Man must undergo great suffering, and be rejected by the elders, chief priests, and
scribes, and be killed, and on the third day be raised."

Then he said to them all, "If any want to become
my followers, let them deny themselves and take up
their cross daily and follow me. For those who want to
save their life will lose it, and those who lose their life
for my sake will save it. What does it profit them if they
gain the whole world, but lose or forfeit themselves?"

Notice what you think and feel as you read the Gospel.

Jesus knew the death he would die and sought to prepare his disciples to carry their own crosses. Those who seek to preserve their lives will lose them. What else do you notice in this Gospel?

Pray as you are led for yourself and others.

"Jesus, I don't want to gain the whole world at the expense of myself. I don't want to gain the whole world and lose you . . ." (Continue in your own words.)

Listen to Jesus.

Take up your cross today and follow me, for a servant is not greater than the master. My cross is my glory. Your cross shall be yours. What else is Jesus saying to you?

Ask God to show you how to live today.

"Jesus, teach me to embrace my crosses, knowing that they are meaningful because of you. I offer my sufferings for the good of those who suffer today. Amen."

Friday, February 12, 2016

Know that God is present with you and ready to converse.

"You are always with me, Jesus, but you are not present to me as you were to your disciples. I seek greater closeness with you."

Read the Gospel: Matthew 9:14–15.

Then the disciples of John came to Jesus, saying, "Why do we and the Pharisees fast often, but your disciples do not fast?" And Jesus said to them, "The wedding guests cannot mourn as long as the bridegroom is with them, can they? The days will come when the bridegroom is taken away from them, and then they will fast."

Notice what you think and feel as you read the Gospel.

When Jesus, the bridegroom, is taken from them, then will his disciples fast.

Pray as you are led for yourself and others.

"Jesus, I wish to fast and pray during this season. I offer my sacrifices for the good of others. How marvelous that fasting and praying accomplish good in this world . . ." (Continue in your own words.)

Listen to Jesus.

When you fast and pray, you imitate me. When you fast and pray, you draw out of yourself and enter into me. I can teach you what you need to know. What else is Jesus saying to you?

Ask God to show you how to live today.

"Help me, Lord. Show me how to do this well. Amen."

Saturday, February 13, 2016

Know that God is present with you and ready to converse.

"You spend time with sinners, Lord. I am one."

Read the Gospel: Luke 5:27–32.

After this Jesus went out and saw a tax collector named Levi, sitting at the tax booth; and he said to him, "Follow me." And he got up, left everything, and followed him.

Then Levi gave a great banquet for him in his house; and there was a large crowd of tax collectors and others sitting at the table with them. The Pharisees and their scribes were complaining to his disciples, saying, "Why do you eat and drink with tax collectors and sinners?" Jesus answered, "Those who are well have no need of a physician, but those who are sick;

I have come to call not the righteous but sinners to repentance."

Notice what you think and feel as you read the Gospel.

Under criticism for fraternizing with tax collectors and sinners, Jesus says he has come to call sinners to repentance.

Pray as you are led for yourself and others.

"Lord, you call me. I come to you repenting . . ." (Continue in your own words.)

Listen to Jesus.

Your sins are covered by my mercy, my beloved. I forgive you and give you power to make amends and avoid those offenses in the future. What else is Jesus saying to you?

Ask God to show you how to live today.

"Jesus, how do I make amends? Amen."

FIRST WEEK OF LENT

The tempter is clever: he does not direct us immediately toward evil but toward a false good,
making us believe that power and things that sati-
ate primary needs are what is most real. In this
manner, God becomes secondary; he is reduced to
a means, he becomes unreal, he no longer counts,
he disappears. . . . In the decisive moments of life . . .
we are faced with a choice: do we want to follow the
'I' or God? Do we want to follow individual interests
or rather the true good?

Pope Benedict XVI

Sunday, February 14, 2016
First Sunday of Lent

**Know that God is present with
you and ready to converse.**

During Lent, we are called to repentance by the words
of Jesus. More than that, we are called to holiness, without
which no one will see God. We must find it in the
Word and be transformed by the Spirit of holiness.

You may begin by opening yourself to the Lord with
words such as these: "Jesus, you overcame temptation
by the Word of God. Be with me in my temptations and
help me overcome them."

Read the Gospel: Luke 4:1–13.

Jesus, full of the Holy Spirit, returned from the Jordan
and was led by the Spirit in the wilderness, where for
forty days he was tempted by the devil. He ate nothing
at all during those days, and when they were over, he
was famished. The devil said to him, "If you are the
Son of God, command this stone to become a loaf of
bread." Jesus answered him, "It is written, 'One does
not live by bread alone.'"

Then the devil led him up and showed him in an
instant all the kingdoms of the world. And the devil
said to him, "To you I will give their glory and all this
authority; for it has been given over to me, and I give
it to anyone I please. If you, then, will worship me, it
will all be yours." Jesus answered him, "It is written,

'Worship the Lord your God,
and serve only him.'"

Then the devil took him to Jerusalem, and placed him on the pinnacle of the Temple, saying to him, "If you are the Son of God, throw yourself down from here, for it is written,

'He will command his angels concerning you,
to protect you,'
and

'On their hands they will bear you up,
so that you will not dash your foot against a stone.'"

Jesus answered him, "It is said, 'Do not put the Lord your God to the test.'" When the devil had finished every test, he departed from him until an opportune time.

Notice what you think and feel as you read the Gospel.

The devil offers Jesus the glory of all the kingdoms of the world in a moment of time, saying they had been delivered to him to give to whomever he wished. What else do you notice in this Gospel?

Pray as you are led for yourself and others.

"Jesus, your kingdom is not of this world. You came to save souls, not to establish an earthly power. In infinite love, you value our souls. Give me that same mind . . ." (Continue in your own words.)

Listen to Jesus.

When you are tempted, cast your mind upon the things of God, all things good and true and beautiful. These are the things that will endure forever. What else is Jesus saying to you?

Ask God to show you how to live today.

"Reveal to me the ways that evil crawls into my life. Make me aware of my temptations and give me grace to resist them. Amen."

Monday, February 15, 2016

Know that God is present with you and ready to converse.

"You are present in the hungry, the thirsty, the stranger, the naked, and the imprisoned. You are also here with me. Teach me, Lord."

Read the Gospel: Matthew 25:31–46.

"When the Son of Man comes in his glory, and all the angels with him, then he will sit on the throne of his glory. All the nations will be gathered before him, and he will separate people one from another as a shepherd separates the sheep from the goats, and he will put the sheep at his right hand and the goats at the left. Then the king will say to those at his right hand, 'Come, you that are blessed by my Father, inherit the kingdom prepared for you from the foundation of the world; for I was hungry and you gave me food, I was thirsty and you gave me something to drink, I was a stranger and you welcomed me, I was naked and you gave me clothing, I was sick and you took care of me, I was in prison and you visited me.' Then the righteous will answer him, 'Lord, when was it that we saw you hungry and gave you food, or thirsty and gave you something to drink? And when was it that we saw you a stranger and welcomed you, or naked and gave you clothing? And when was it that we saw you sick or in prison and visited you?' And the king will answer them, 'Truly I tell you, just as you did it to one of the least of these who are members of my family, you did it to me.' Then he will say to those at his left hand, 'You that are accursed, depart from me into the eternal fire prepared for the devil and his angels; for I was hungry and you gave me no food, I was thirsty and you gave me nothing to drink, I was a stranger and you did not welcome me, naked and you did not give me clothing, sick and in prison and you did not visit me.' Then they also will answer, 'Lord, when was it that we saw you hungry or thirsty or a stranger or naked or sick or in prison, and did not take care of you?' Then he will answer them, 'Truly I tell you, just as you did not do it to one of the least of these, you did not do it to me.' And these will go away into eternal punishment, but the righteous into eternal life."

Notice what you think and feel as you read the Gospel.

You are judging the nations, Jesus, and you are judging us all. You judge humankind on the basis of what we have done for those in need; for what we do for the least of these, we do to you.

Pray as you are led for yourself and others.

"You challenge me, Jesus, for I seem to be more occupied with ignoring the needy than with helping them. I sometimes forget the poor and hurting, or think that somehow they don't involve me. But they do, for you are there in the faces of the poor . . ." (Continue in your own words.)

Listen to Jesus.

I am truly present in the poor, the sick, the suffering, the homeless, and the imprisoned. It is not your place to judge them, for they are victims. For my sake, have compassion on them and do what you can to help them. What else is Jesus saying to you?

Ask God to show you how to live today.

"Jesus, your kingdom in the making is glorious, for you love us all, even me. Help me to act on what I know to your honor and glory. Amen."

Tuesday, February 16, 2016

Know that God is present with you and ready to converse.

"Father in heaven, you are here with me. I open myself to your Word, Jesus."

Read the Gospel: Matthew 6:7–15.

Jesus instructed, "When you are praying, do not heap up empty phrases as the Gentiles do; for they think that they will be heard because of their many words. Do not be like them, for your Father knows what you need before you ask him.

"Pray then in this way:

Our Father in heaven,
hallowed be your name.
Your kingdom come.
Your will be done,
on earth as it is in heaven.
Give us this day our daily bread.
And forgive us our debts,
as we also have forgiven our debtors.
And do not bring us to the time of trial,
but rescue us from the evil one.

"For if you forgive others their trespasses, your heavenly Father will also forgive you; but if you do not forgive others, neither will your Father forgive your trespasses."

Notice what you think and feel as you read the Gospel.

How do we get through to God? He is not impressed by our piling up many words of prayers. Nor do we need to beg God for what we need. Instead, God and forgiveness are found when we forgive others.

Pray as you are led for yourself and others.

"Our Father, who art in heaven . . ." (Continue in your own words.)

Listen to Jesus.

Do you lack forgiveness in your life, in your heart, dear one? Can you forgive? Forgiveness can be difficult. But this is the way to God. What else is Jesus saying to you?

Ask God to show you how to live today.

"Lord, I don't want just to go through the motions of forgiving someone who has trespassed against me. I want to forgive that person completely from my heart. Then I can put that hurt behind me forever. Help me. Amen."

Wednesday, February 17, 2016

**Know that God is present with
you and ready to converse.**

"Something greater than Solomon is here, Lord. You
are here now. I will listen to your Word."

Read the Gospel: Luke 11:29–32.

When the crowds were increasing, Jesus began to say,
"This generation is an evil generation; it asks for a
sign, but no sign will be given to it except the sign of
Jonah. For just as Jonah became a sign to the people
of Nineveh, so the Son of Man will be to this generation. The queen of the south will rise at the judgment
with the people of this generation and condemn them,
because she came from the ends of the earth to listen
to the wisdom of Solomon, and see, something greater
than Solomon is here! The people of Nineveh will rise
up at the judgment with this generation and condemn
it, because they repented at the proclamation of Jonah,
and see, something greater than Jonah is here!"

Notice what you think and feel
as you read the Gospel.

Jesus knows the hearts of humans. He knows our
self-interest. He knows our desire for signs and proofs
that he is the Messiah. He cannot win over the skeptics
no matter what he does.

Pray as you are led for yourself and others.

"Jesus, I do not want to be part of an evil generation, challenging you, doubting you. I want . . ." (Continue in your own words.)

Listen to Jesus.

I want what's best for you, my child and friend. People often hold on to habits of sin because they think they cannot live without them. I tell you truly that you will be happier without them. What else is Jesus saying to you?

Ask God to show you how to live today.

"Lord, I bow before you. Heal me. Lift me up to serve you and those you give to me. Amen."

Thursday, February 18, 2016

Know that God is present with you and ready to converse.

"I seek you, Lord, but you are already found. And you find me here now, ready to be with you."

Read the Gospel: Matthew 7:7–12.

Jesus instructed, "Ask, and it will be given you; search, and you will find; knock, and the door will be opened for you. For everyone who asks receives, and everyone who searches finds, and for everyone who knocks, the door will be opened. Is there anyone among you who, if your child asks for bread, will give a stone? Or if the child asks for a fish, will give a snake? If you then, who are evil, know how to give good gifts to your children, how much more will your Father in heaven give good things to those who ask him!

"In everything do to others as you would have them do to you; for this is the law and the prophets."

Notice what you think and feel as you read the Gospel.

Jesus is teaching. How we judge others determines how we are judged. Rather than look at others' faults, we should look at our own. What we desire and seek from God we receive, for God is good. What else do you notice in this Gospel?

Pray as you are led for yourself and others.

"Lord, forgive me for judging others, forgive my hypocrisies, and forgive me for not doing unto others what I would have others do to me . . ." (Continue in your own words.)

Listen to Jesus.

I grant you what you seek, my child. Ask me now for whatever you want from God for yourself and for others. What else is Jesus saying to you?

Ask God to show you how to live today.

"Lord, alert me when you see me begin to judge someone else, and turn me toward you. I give you this day.
I need you. Amen."

Friday, February 19, 2016

**Know that God is present with
you and ready to converse.**

"The Word of God is before me. Jesus is present in
Word and in Spirit. Open my heart, Lord."

Read the Gospel: Matthew 5:20–26.

Jesus said, "For I tell you, unless your righteousness
exceeds that of the scribes and Pharisees, you will
never enter the kingdom of heaven.

"You have heard that it was said to those of ancient
times, 'You shall not murder'; and 'whoever murders
shall be liable to judgment.' But I say to you that if you
are angry with a brother or sister, you will be liable to
judgment; and if you insult a brother or sister, you will
be liable to the council; and if you say, 'You fool,' you
will be liable to the hell of fire. So when you are offering your gift at the altar, if you remember that your
brother or sister has something against you, leave your
gift there before the altar and go; first be reconciled to
your brother or sister, and then come and offer your
gift. Come to terms quickly with your accuser while
you are on the way to court with him, or your accuser

may hand you over to the judge, and the judge to the guard, and you will be thrown into prison. Truly I tell you, you will never get out until you have paid the last penny."

Notice what you think and feel as you read the Gospel.

Jesus emphasizes the importance of moral behavior in our dealings with others. Little things are important. Rudeness and anger toward another violate God's commandment. Do not allow someone to hold a grudge against you, Jesus says. Resolving a human dispute is more important than making an offering to God.

Pray as you are led for yourself and others.

"Jesus, you set moral standards higher than the scribes and Pharisees. Who can stand before you? Wash me and lead me in the way of holiness . . ." (Continue in your own words.)

Listen to Jesus.

My child, I am working in you. I desire your holiness. Take a moment now to consider who may need to forgive you. What can you do to reconcile? What else is Jesus saying to you?

Ask God to show you how to live today.

Lord, you ask much. Give me grace, strength, and courage to do what you ask. Amen."

Saturday, February 20, 2016

**Know that God is present with
you and ready to converse.**

"Heavenly Father, rain down your love upon me as I attend to your Word, my Lord and Savior, your Son, Jesus. "

Read the Gospel: Matthew 5:43–48.

Jesus said, "You have heard that it was said, 'You shall love your neighbor and hate your enemy.' But I say to you, love your enemies and pray for those who persecute you, so that you may be children of your Father in heaven; for he makes his sun rise on the evil and on the good, and sends rain on the righteous and on the unrighteous. For if you love those who love you, what reward do you have? Do not even the tax collectors do the same? And if you greet only your brothers and sisters, what more are you doing than others? Do not even the Gentiles do the same? Be perfect, therefore, as your heavenly Father is perfect."

**Notice what you think and feel
as you read the Gospel.**

Jesus asks us to be perfect, and he also says how we can achieve it: by loving our enemies as well as our family and friends.

Pray as you are led for yourself and others.

"Lord, whom do I hate, dislike, criticize, avoid, or fear? Bring these people to my mind. Put your love for them into my heart . . ." (Continue in your own words.)

Listen to Jesus.

Dear friend, do you see that my way of love is the way to peace and joy? It is also the way of healing and wholeness. Love all people and see the world change around you. What else is Jesus saying to you?

Ask God to show you how to live today.

"Lord, you have given me an assignment today, an exercise in holiness, an exercise of the heart. Give me your heart as I seek to love people that I have forgotten to love. Amen."

SECOND WEEK OF LENT

Saint Augustine points out that only God, as the supreme good, is capable of overcoming the various forms of poverty present in our world. Mercy and love for one's neighbor must therefore be the fruit of a living relationship with God and have God as their constant point of reference, since it is in closeness to Christ that we find our joy.

Saint John Paul II

Sunday, February 21, 2016
Second Sunday of Lent

**Know that God is present with
you and ready to converse.**

Jesus was present with Moses and Elijah on the mountain. He was present with Peter, James, and John. He was present with the multitudes. He is present with you now.

When you are ready, invite God to speak to you with words such as these: "Thank you for loving me, Lord. I long to see your glory."

Read the Gospel: Luke 9:28b–36.

Jesus took with him Peter and John and James, and went up on the mountain to pray. And while he was praying, the appearance of his face changed, and his clothes became dazzling white. Suddenly they saw two men, Moses and Elijah, talking to him. They appeared in glory and were speaking of his departure, which he was about to accomplish at Jerusalem. Now Peter and his companions were weighed down with sleep; but since they had stayed awake, they saw his glory and the two men who stood with him. Just as they were leaving him, Peter said to Jesus, "Master, it is good for us to be here; let us make three dwellings, one for you, one for Moses, and one for Elijah"—not knowing what he said. While he was saying this, a cloud came and overshadowed them; and they were terrified as they entered the cloud. Then from the cloud came a voice that said, "This is my Son, my Chosen; listen to him!" When the voice had spoken, Jesus was found alone. And they kept silent and in those days told no one any of the things they had seen.

Notice what you think and feel as you read the Gospel.

How fortunate for the disciples to see Jesus transfigured while praying on the mountain and talking with Moses and Elijah. They are talking about Jesus' "departure, which he was about to accomplish at Jerusalem." What is Jesus saying to them? What are they saying to Jesus?

Pray as you are led for yourself and others.

"Lord, you came into this world to depart from it in a violent death, imposed upon you by those you loved and came to save. I love you for that. Let the power of your love live in me . . ." (Continue in your own words.)

Listen to Jesus.

You read about Moses, Elijah, and me revealed in glory. My disciples were in awe. The kingdom of heaven is far beyond whatever glory you can imagine now. I look forward to the day when I can reveal its glory to you. What else is Jesus saying to you?

Ask God to show you how to live today.

"Peter wanted to build three booths to honor Jesus and the prophets. How may I honor you today, Jesus? For you are the Son of God. Amen."

Monday, February 22, 2016
Chair of Saint Peter

Know that God is present with you and ready to converse.

"Word of the Father, I joyfully come into your presence to love you, know you, and serve you."

Read the Gospel: Matthew 16:13–19.

Now when Jesus came into the district of Caesarea Philippi, he asked his disciples, "Who do people say that the Son of Man is?" And they said, "Some say John the Baptist, but others Elijah, and still others Jeremiah or one of the prophets." He said to them, "But who do you say that I am?" Simon Peter answered, "You are the Messiah, the Son of the living God." And Jesus answered him, "Blessed are you, Simon son of Jonah! For flesh and blood has not revealed this to you, but my Father in heaven. And I tell you, you are Peter, and on this rock I will build my Church, and the gates of Hades will not prevail against it. I will give you the keys of the kingdom of heaven, and whatever you bind on earth will be bound in heaven, and whatever you loose on earth will be loosed in heaven."

Notice what you think and feel as you read the Gospel.

Jesus affirms that he is the Christ and proclaims to Peter that he is the rock upon which he will build his Church. Peter is to receive the keys of the kingdom of heaven—powers in heaven and on earth.

Pray as you are led for yourself and others.

"Lord, you are true to your word. Against all odds your Church continues to this day, and it will continue until you return. I pray for your Church and all who serve in it, that they may do so with the love, wisdom, and power that comes by your Spirit . . ." (Continue in your own words.)

Listen to Jesus.

You, too, belong to my Church, which is my Body. I ask my followers to love one another so the world will know that I am among you. What else is Jesus saying to you?

Ask God to show you how to live today.

"Jesus, how may I help to unify those who follow you? Amen."

Tuesday, February 23, 2016

**Know that God is present with
you and ready to converse.**

"I am here, Lord. Open my heart to your Word."

**Read the Gospel: Matthew
23:1–12* (1–3, 8–12).**

Then Jesus said to the crowds and to his disciples, "The
scribes and the Pharisees sit on Moses' seat; therefore,
do whatever they teach you and follow it; but do not
do as they do, for they do not practice what they teach.
. . . But you are not to be called rabbi, for you have one
teacher, and you are all students. And call no one your
father on earth, for you have one Father—the one in
heaven. Nor are you to be called instructors, for you
have one instructor, the Messiah. The greatest among
you will be your servant. All who exalt themselves
will be humbled, and all who humble themselves will
be exalted."

**Notice what you think and feel
as you read the Gospel.**

Jesus says that earthly distinctions, appearance, rank,
and status are not the way God sees us. If we aspire to
greatness, we should be servants.

Pray as you are led for yourself and others.

"Jesus, you came to serve us, the great and small. Your amazing words and your amazing deeds proclaim the truth. I give myself to you today as your humble servant . . ." (Continue in your own words.)

Listen to Jesus.

There is joy in serving others, my beloved. I want you to know joy as I know it. What else is Jesus saying to you?

Ask God to show you how to live today.

"Jesus, let my love for you translate into actions in my day. I need you to walk with me and guide me in all things. Amen."

Wednesday, February 24, 2016

Know that God is present with you and ready to converse.

"Lord, please don't let me hear your Word and be oblivious to what you are saying to me. Elevate my heart and mind to receive you."

Read the Gospel: Matthew 20:17–28* (20–28).

Then the mother of the sons of Zebedee came to Jesus with her sons, and kneeling before him, she asked a favor of him. And he said to her, "What do you want?" She said to him, "Declare that these two sons of mine will sit, one at your right hand and one at your left, in your kingdom." But Jesus answered, "You do not know what you are asking. Are you able to drink the cup that I am about to drink?" They said to him, "We are able." He said to them, "You will indeed drink my cup, but to sit at my right hand and at my left, this is not mine to grant, but it is for those for whom it has been prepared by my Father."

When the ten heard it, they were angry with the two brothers. But Jesus called them to him and said, "You know that the rulers of the Gentiles lord it over them, and their great ones are tyrants over them. It will not be so among you; but whoever wishes to be great among you must be your servant, and whoever wishes to be first among you must be your slave; just as the Son of Man came not to be served but to serve, and to give his life as a ransom for many."

Notice what you think and feel as you read the Gospel.

Jesus tells the Twelve exactly what's going to happen to him in Jerusalem: his passion, death, and resurrection on the third day. What did his disciples understand? They are concerned about their status when he comes into his kingdom. What else do you notice?

Pray as you are led for yourself and others.

"Lord, I guess it is human nature that we want honor and power for ourselves. Thank you for reminding me again that greatness is acquired by serving others. Show me how . . ." (Continue in your own words.)

Listen to Jesus.

Whom can you serve, my dear disciple? The one you serve today will be me. What else is Jesus saying to you?

Ask God to show you how to live today.

"Lord, walking in your humble way is challenging. You ask me to be better than I have ever been. I can accomplish none of it without you. Be with me today. Amen."

Thursday, February 25, 2016

Know that God is present with you and ready to converse.

"Give me ears to hear your Word, Lord, for you are with me."

Read the Gospel: Luke 16:19–31.

Jesus taught, "There was a rich man who was dressed in purple and fine linen and who feasted sumptuously every day. And at his gate lay a poor man named Lazarus, covered with sores, who longed to satisfy his hunger with what fell from the rich man's table; even the dogs would come and lick his sores. The poor man died and was carried away by the angels to be with Abraham. The rich man also died and was buried. In

Hades, where he was being tormented, he looked up
and saw Abraham far away with Lazarus by his side.
He called out, 'Father Abraham, have mercy on me,
and send Lazarus to dip the tip of his finger in water
and cool my tongue; for I am in agony in these flames.'
But Abraham said, 'Child, remember that during your
lifetime you received your good things, and Lazarus
in like manner evil things; but now he is comforted
here, and you are in agony. Besides all this, between
you and us a great chasm has been fixed, so that those
who might want to pass from here to you cannot do
so, and no one can cross from there to us.' He said,
'Then, father, I beg you to send him to my father's
house—for I have five brothers—that he may warn
them, so that they will not also come into this place
of torment.' Abraham replied, 'They have Moses and
the prophets; they should listen to them.' He said, 'No,
father Abraham; but if someone goes to them from the
dead, they will repent.' He said to him, 'If they do not
listen to Moses and the prophets, neither will they be
convinced even if someone rises from the dead.'"

Notice what you think and feel as you read the Gospel.

In the parable of the rich man and poor Lazarus, Jesus
connects human behavior in life to final destiny after
death. The twist is that Jesus says that many people
ignore the messages of the prophets, even the prophet
who rose from the dead.

Pray as you are led for yourself and others.

"I desire to receive your words today, risen Lord, and to take them to heart. Lead me to upright behavior and compassionate acts . . ." (Continue in your own words.)

Listen to Jesus.

It is very pleasant to spend time with you, beloved. You are mine and I am yours. What would you like from me? What else is Jesus saying to you?

Ask God to show you how to live today.

"Jesus, you are good to me. Is there a Lazarus in my life whom I can help? Amen."

Friday, February 26, 2016

Know that God is present with you and ready to converse.

"Let me not be one of those who resist your Word, Lord. I wish to live by every word that proceeds from the mouth of God."

Read the Gospel: Matthew 21:33–43, 45–46* (33–43).

Jesus, "Listen to another parable. There was a landowner who planted a vineyard, put a fence around it, dug a wine press in it, and built a watchtower. Then he leased it to tenants and went to another country.

When the harvest time had come, he sent his slaves to the tenants to collect his produce. But the tenants seized his slaves and beat one, killed another, and stoned another. Again he sent other slaves, more than the first; and they treated them in the same way. Finally he sent his son to them, saying, 'They will respect my son.' But when the tenants saw the son, they said to themselves, 'This is the heir; come, let us kill him and get his inheritance.' So they seized him, threw him out of the vineyard, and killed him. Now when the owner of the vineyard comes, what will he do to those tenants?" They said to him, "He will put those wretches to a miserable death, and lease the vineyard to other tenants who will give him the produce at the harvest time."

Jesus said to them, "Have you never read in the scriptures:

'The stone that the builders rejected
    has become the cornerstone;
this was the Lord's doing,
    and it is amazing in our eyes'?

"Therefore I tell you, the kingdom of God will be taken away from you and given to a people that produces the fruits of the kingdom."

Notice what you think and feel as you read the Gospel.

Jesus tells his own story in this parable of the unjust tenants, and he foretells his own end at the hands of those who reject him. They will kill him, yet the very stone that the builders rejected has become the head of the corner.

Pray as you are led for yourself and others.

"Your words and your ways are marvelous, Jesus, and you are my rock, the stone at the corner of my life . . ." (Continue in your own words.)

Listen to Jesus.

I am happy when you speak to me, listen to me, and follow my motives and desires. For I wish no one ill. Let us be close and embrace all others. What else is Jesus saying to you?

Ask God to show you how to live today.

"As friends, Jesus, we go out together into the world, living your good news, sharing it with everyone. Let me not be afraid of rejection. Amen."

Saturday, February 27, 2016

Know that God is present with you and ready to converse.

"Good Shepherd, when I am lost, you find me; when I come back to you seeking forgiveness, you welcome me. You are above all human praise."

Read the Gospel: Luke 15:1–3, 11–32* (11–32).

Then Jesus said, "There was a man who had two sons. The younger of them said to his father, 'Father, give me the share of the property that will belong to me.' So he divided his property between them. A few days later the younger son gathered all he had and traveled to a distant country, and there he squandered his property in dissolute living. When he had spent everything, a severe famine took place throughout that country, and he began to be in need. So he went and hired himself out to one of the citizens of that country, who sent him to his fields to feed the pigs. He would gladly have filled himself with the pods that the pigs were eating; and no one gave him anything. But when he came to himself he said, 'How many of my father's hired hands have bread enough and to spare, but here I am dying of hunger! I will get up and go to my father, and I will say to him, "Father, I have sinned against heaven and before you; I am no longer worthy to be called your son; treat me like one of your hired hands."' So he set off and went to his father. But while he was still far off, his father saw him and was filled with compassion; he ran and put his arms around him and kissed him. Then the son said to him, 'Father, I have sinned against heaven and before you; I am no longer worthy to be called your son.' But the father said to his slaves, 'Quickly, bring out a robe—the best one—and put it on him; put a ring on his finger and sandals on his feet. And get the fatted calf and kill it, and let us eat and celebrate; for this son of mine was dead and is alive again; he was lost and is found!' And they began to celebrate.

"Now his elder son was in the field; and when he came and approached the house, he heard music and dancing. He called one of the slaves and asked what was going on. He replied, 'Your brother has come, and your father has killed the fatted calf, because he has got him back safe and sound.' Then he became angry and refused to go in. His father came out and began to plead with him. But he answered his father, 'Listen! For all these years I have been working like a slave for you, and I have never disobeyed your command; yet you have never given me even a young goat so that I might celebrate with my friends. But when this son of yours came back, who has devoured your property with prostitutes, you killed the fatted calf for him!' Then the father said to him, 'Son, you are always with me, and all that is mine is yours. But we had to celebrate and rejoice, because this brother of yours was dead and has come to life; he was lost and has been found.'"

Notice what you think and feel as you read the Gospel.

Jesus speaks of his Father and himself in this great parable of the prodigal son. The younger son has learned a lesson. What does the older son learn?

Pray as you are led for yourself and others.

"Jesus, you know the human heart. You know me inside and out. I am created for you. Help me fulfill my destiny. Lead me in your way of love for others. I pray for . . ." (Continue in your own words.)

Listen to Jesus.

I hear your prayers, dear one. I am like a father or a mother who wants only what is best for you. What else is Jesus saying to you?

Ask God to show you how to live today.

"We have spent time together, Lord. Let me go forth to do unto others as I would have them do unto me. With your help, nothing is impossible. Amen."

THIRD WEEK OF LENT

In the presence of Christ man is illumined with a new light and consequently recognizes the holiness of God and the gravity of sin. Through the Word of Christ a message is transmitted to him that invites him to conversion and grants forgiveness of sins. These gifts he fully attains in baptism. This sacrament, in fact, configures him to the passion, death, and resurrection of the Lord and places the whole future of the life of the baptized under the seal of this mystery.

Blessed Paul VI

Sunday, February 28, 2016
Third Sunday of Lent

Know that God is present with you and ready to converse.

Jesus preached against judging others. We need humility to walk in his way.

When you are ready to hear his voice in the Word, invite him to teach you in words such as these: "Lord, the world can be a frightening place, with violence, accidents, and disasters. Let me trust you when I am afraid. Let me trust you now."

Read the Gospel: Luke 13:1–9* (1–5).

At that very time there were some present who told Jesus about the Galileans whose blood Pilate had mingled with their sacrifices. He asked them, "Do you think that because these Galileans suffered in this way they were worse sinners than all other Galileans? No, I tell you; but unless you repent, you will all perish as they did. Or those eighteen who were killed when the tower of Siloam fell on them—do you think that they were worse offenders than all the others living in Jerusalem? No, I tell you; but unless you repent, you will all perish just as they did."

Notice what you think and feel as you read the Gospel.

Jesus cautions us against judging victims of violence in any form. We are not here to judge but to get right with God.

Pray as you are led for yourself and others.

"Lord, I pray for all victims. I hear about them in the news of the world, the nation, and my community. No one deserves to be a victim. You were a victim, Lamb of God, and you had a purpose. Accomplish your purposes now. Send me . . ." (Continue in your own words.)

Listen to Jesus.

I want you to be fruitful, my beloved, because the world needs those who care for others, who aid those in need, speak the truth, and work for justice. What else is Jesus saying to you?

Ask God to show you how to live today.

"Today I offer myself as a living sacrifice. This is how I choose to worship you, Lord. Make of me what you will. Amen."

Monday, February 29, 2016

Know that God is present with you and ready to converse.

"You go to people who are not your own. You speak to sinners. You are here with me. Let me hear your Word, Lord."

Read the Gospel: John 4:5–42* (5–26).

So Jesus came to a Samaritan city called Sychar, near the plot of ground that Jacob had given to his son Joseph. Jacob's well was there, and Jesus, tired out by his journey, was sitting by the well. It was about noon.

A Samaritan woman came to draw water, and Jesus said to her, "Give me a drink." (His disciples had gone to the city to buy food.) The Samaritan woman said to him, "How is it that you, a Jew, ask a drink of me, a woman of Samaria?" (Jews do not share things in common with Samaritans.) Jesus answered her, "If you knew the gift of God, and who it is that is saying to you, 'Give me a drink,' you would have asked him, and he would have given you living water." The woman said to him, "Sir, you have no bucket, and the well is deep. Where do you get that living water? Are you greater than our ancestor Jacob, who gave us the well, and with his sons and his flocks drank from it?" Jesus said to her, "Everyone who drinks of this water will be thirsty again, but those who drink of the water that I will give them will never be thirsty. The water that I will give will become in them a spring of water gushing up to eternal life." The woman said to him, "Sir, give me this water, so that I may never be thirsty or have to keep coming here to draw water."

Jesus said to her, "Go, call your husband, and come back." The woman answered him, "I have no husband." Jesus said to her, "You are right in saying, 'I have no husband'; for you have had five husbands, and the one you have now is not your husband. What you have said is true!" The woman said to him, "Sir, I see that you are a prophet. Our ancestors worshiped on this mountain, but you say that the place where people must worship is in Jerusalem." Jesus said to her, "Woman, believe me, the hour is coming when you will worship the Father neither on this mountain nor in Jerusalem. You worship what you do not know; we worship what we know, for salvation is from the Jews. But the hour is coming, and is now here, when the true worshipers will worship the Father in spirit and truth, for the Father seeks such as these to worship him. God is spirit, and those who worship him must worship in spirit and truth." The woman said to him, "I know that Messiah is coming" (who is called Christ). "When he comes, he will proclaim all things to us." Jesus said to her, "I am he, the one who is speaking to you."

Notice what you think and feel as you read the Gospel.

This passage is a short story with setting, characters, and dialogue. The theme is that Jesus is the Christ, the Savior of the world, for those who receive him in spirit and in truth. Do you identify with the woman at the well?

Pray as you are led for yourself and others.

"Lord Jesus, you came for all people, especially those far from God. I cannot thank you enough. The world cannot glorify you enough. I have springs of living water within me. How may I channel them to others?" (Continue in your own words.)

Listen to Jesus.

The secret to bearing fruit, helping others, is to abide in me. Ours is the key relationship. It's like a good marriage. Everything else will follow. What else is Jesus saying to you?

Ask God to show you how to live today.

"Jesus, I have little idea what is good, what is best, what is your will for me. Show me, enable me, and let it glorify you. Amen."

Tuesday, March 1, 2016

Know that God is present with you and ready to converse.

"God, great Lord of hosts, you are waiting for me to open my mind and my heart to your Word, Jesus, your Son and my Savior. Praise him!"

Read the Gospel: Matthew 18:21–35* (22–35).

Jesus said, "For this reason the kingdom of heaven may be compared to a king who wished to settle accounts with his slaves. When he began the reckoning, one who owed him ten thousand talents was brought to him; and, as he could not pay, his lord ordered him to be sold, together with his wife and children and all his possessions, and payment to be made. So the slave fell on his knees before him, saying, 'Have patience with me, and I will pay you everything.' And out of pity for him, the lord of that slave released him and forgave him the debt. But that same slave, as he went out, came upon one of his fellow slaves who owed him a hundred denarii; and seizing him by the throat, he said, 'Pay what you owe.' Then his fellow slave fell down and pleaded with him, 'Have patience with me, and I will pay you.' But he refused; then he went and threw him into prison until he would pay the debt. When his fellow slaves saw what had happened, they were greatly distressed, and they went and reported to their lord all that had taken place. Then his lord summoned him and said to him, 'You wicked slave! I forgave you all that debt because you pleaded with me. Should you not have had mercy on your fellow slave, as I had mercy on you?' And in anger his lord handed him over to be tortured until he would pay his entire debt. So my heavenly Father will also do to every one of you, if you do not forgive your brother or sister from your heart."

Notice what you think and feel as you read the Gospel.

The master forgives his servant's large debt, but the servant will not forgive a much smaller debt of a fellow servant. Angry, the master delivers the unforgiving servant to jail. Jesus says his Father will do the same to us unless we forgive our brothers from our hearts.

Pray as you are led for yourself and others.

"Lord, this parable ends in justice. But that justice is related to mercy. God has mercy on me and forgives me. So I must do the same . . ." (Continue in your own words.)

Listen to Jesus.

It's a law of grace, my child, that you receive mercy as you extend mercy to those who offend you. What else is Jesus saying to you?

Ask God to show you how to live today.

"Lord, what can I do today to make up for grudges I have harbored for hurts and slights I have received from others? I wish to be free of unforgiveness. Amen."

Wednesday, March 2, 2016

Know that God is present with you and ready to converse.

"Lord, let your Word be my law. I am ready to hear you now."

Read the Gospel: Matthew 5:17–19.

Jesus said, "Do not think that I have come to abolish the law or the prophets; I have come not to abolish but to fulfill. For truly I tell you, until heaven and earth pass away, not one letter, not one stroke of a letter, will pass from the law until all is accomplished. Therefore, whoever breaks one of the least of these commandments, and teaches others to do the same, will be called least in the kingdom of heaven; but whoever does them and teaches them will be called great in the kingdom of heaven."

**Notice what you think and feel
as you read the Gospel.**

Jesus came not to abolish but to fulfill the law and the prophets. We are to take the commandments seriously and teach others to do the same.

Pray as you are led for yourself and others.

"Lord, you know my heart. I want to obey you because I want to please you in all I think, say, and do . . ." (Continue in your own words.)

Listen to Jesus.

Repentance is a spring of renewal, my child. I hear your confession. I absolve you of your sin. What else is Jesus saying to you?

Ask God to show you how to live today.

"Lord, how may I give alms today? I want to show my gratitude to you for your mercy. Amen."

Thursday, March 3, 2016

**Know that God is present with
you and ready to converse.**

"Jesus, I am with you. Keep me close."

Read the Gospel: Luke 11:14–23* (14–20, 23).

Now Jesus was casting out a demon that was mute; when the demon had gone out, the one who had been mute spoke, and the crowds were amazed. But some of them said, "He casts out demons by Beelzebul, the ruler of the demons." Others, to test him, kept demanding from him a sign from heaven. But he knew what they were thinking and said to them, "Every kingdom divided against itself becomes a desert, and house falls on house. If Satan also is divided against himself, how will his kingdom stand? For you say that I cast out the demons by Beelzebul. Now if I cast out the demons by Beelzebul, by whom do your exorcists cast them out? Therefore they will be your judges. But if it is by the finger of God that I cast out the demons, then the kingdom of God has come to you. . . . Whoever is not with me is against me, and whoever does not gather with me scatters."

Notice what you think and feel as you read the Gospel.

In response to criticism, Jesus affirms that his authority over demons comes from God, not Beelzebul. He says that the one who does not gather with him scatters.

Pray as you are led for yourself and others.

"Dear Jesus, I gather. I have had enough of scattering. I pray for the many I know who have scattered. Draw them back to you . . ." (Continue in your own words.)

Listen to Jesus.

I care for those who are scattered, too, dear friend. I do not cease to seek them. What else is Jesus saying to you?

Ask God to show you how to live today.

"As I give you my whole self, Lord, show me what to do today for your glory. Amen."

Friday, March 4, 2016

Know that God is present with you and ready to converse.

"Breathe on me, Holy Spirit, outside and inside, heart and mind and soul, and through the Word of God."

Read the Gospel: Matthew 12:28–34* (28–32).

Jesus said, "But if it is by the Spirit of God that I cast out demons, then the kingdom of God has come to you. Or how can one enter a strong man's house and plunder his property, without first tying up the strong man? Then indeed the house can be plundered. Whoever is not with me is against me, and whoever does not gather with me scatters. Therefore I tell you, people will be forgiven for every sin and blasphemy, but blasphemy against the Spirit will not be forgiven. Whoever speaks a word against the Son of Man will be forgiven, but whoever speaks against the Holy Spirit will not be forgiven, either in this age or in the age to come."

Notice what you think and feel as you read the Gospel.

Jesus says he has power by the Holy Spirit and warns those who speak against the Spirit. Jesus shows profound understanding of spiritual realities.

Pray as you are led for yourself and others.

"Lord, I am no better than those you sternly warn. I depend on you to make me good and pleasing to you . . ." (Continue in your own words.)

Listen to Jesus.

I want you to be holy, and I can help you become holy. Come to me often, child. What else is Jesus saying to you?

Ask God to show you how to live today.

"Make me mindful of opportunities to show kindness and fairness all through the day, Lord. Amen."

Saturday, March 5, 2016

Know that God is present with you and ready to converse.

"I come into your presence humbly, Lord, exalting you."

Read the Gospel: Luke 18:9–14.

Jesus also told this parable to some who trusted in themselves that they were righteous and regarded others with contempt: "Two men went up to the Temple to pray, one a Pharisee and the other a tax collector. The Pharisee, standing by himself, was praying thus, 'God, I thank you that I am not like other people: thieves, rogues, adulterers, or even like this tax collector. I fast twice a week; I give a tenth of all my income.' But the tax collector, standing far off, would not even look up to heaven, but was beating his breast and saying, 'God, be merciful to me, a sinner!' I tell you, this man went down to his home justified rather than the other; for all who exalt themselves will be humbled, but all who humble themselves will be exalted."

Notice what you think and feel as you read the Gospel.

Presumably the Pharisee did practice his religion, while the tax collector did not. Yet the Pharisee falls short in his prayer, while the tax collector is justified. What makes the difference here?

Pray as you are led for yourself and others.

"The righteous are prone to spiritual pride. Lord, help me avoid this grievous fault. Let me not find fault in others but rather have true humility . . ." (Continue in your own words.)

Listen to Jesus.

Learn from me because I am meek and lowly of heart, my child. You will be exalted for your humility. What else is Jesus saying to you?

Ask God to show you how to live today.

"Is there someone I can lift up today by some common act of service? Amen."

FOURTH WEEK OF LENT

Consult not your fears but your hopes and dreams. Think not about your frustrations but about your unfulfilled potential. Concern yourself not with what you tried and failed in but with what it is still possible for you to do.

Saint John XXIII

Sunday, March 6, 2016
Fourth Sunday of Lent

**Know that God is present with
you and ready to converse.**

As the prodigal son is welcomed by his father, so we
are welcomed each time we return to God. We turn our
hearts to our loving Father today.

When you are ready, begin: "Father, you are present
in this parable; you are always present in the Word. Let
me be present, too."

Read the Gospel: Luke 15:1–3,
11–32* (11–14, 17–32).

Then Jesus said, "There was a man who had two sons.
The younger of them said to his father, 'Father, give me
the share of the property that will belong to me.' So he
divided his property between them. A few days later
the younger son gathered all he had and traveled to a
distant country, and there he squandered his property
in dissolute living. When he had spent everything, a
severe famine took place throughout that country, and
he began to be in need. . . . But when he came to himself
he said, 'How many of my father's hired hands have
bread enough and to spare, but here I am dying of hunger! I will get up and go to my father, and I will say to
him, "Father, I have sinned against heaven and before
you; I am no longer worthy to be called your son; treat
me like one of your hired hands."' So he set off and

went to his father. But while he was still far off, his father saw him and was filled with compassion; he ran and put his arms around him and kissed him. Then the son said to him, 'Father, I have sinned against heaven and before you; I am no longer worthy to be called your son.' But the father said to his slaves, 'Quickly, bring out a robe—the best one—and put it on him; put a ring on his finger and sandals on his feet. And get the fatted calf and kill it, and let us eat and celebrate; for this son of mine was dead and is alive again; he was lost and is found!' And they began to celebrate.

"Now his elder son was in the field; and when he came and approached the house, he heard music and dancing. He called one of the slaves and asked what was going on. He replied, 'Your brother has come, and your father has killed the fatted calf, because he has got him back safe and sound.' Then he became angry and refused to go in. His father came out and began to plead with him. But he answered his father, 'Listen! For all these years I have been working like a slave for you, and I have never disobeyed your command; yet you have never given me even a young goat so that I might celebrate with my friends. But when this son of yours came back, who has devoured your property with prostitutes, you killed the fatted calf for him!' Then the father said to him, 'Son, you are always with me, and all that is mine is yours. But we had to celebrate and rejoice, because this brother of yours was dead and has come to life; he was lost and has been found.'"

Notice what you think and feel as you read the Gospel.

Jesus tells a story that rings true today with familiar characters: the foolish younger son, the loving and merciful father, and the jealous older son.

Pray as you are led for yourself and others.

"Father, help me come to my senses as the prodigal son did and return home to you as often as I need to. Help others also experience the joy of confessing their sins and receiving forgiveness from God and from those they have injured. I think of . . ." (Continue in your own words.)

Listen to Jesus.

I too want people to reconcile with God. That is the most important thing. Thank you for sharing my desire and praying for others. What else is Jesus saying to you?

Ask God to show you how to live today.

"Have I been waiting for someone who holds something against me to come to me and make peace? Perhaps I can take the initiative in reconciling. Give me wisdom, Jesus. Amen."

Monday, March 7, 2016

**Know that God is present with
you and ready to converse.**

"I invite you to come where you are already, Lord—
here with me. Open my eyes to see you in your Word."

Read the Gospel: John 9:1–41* (1–12).

As he walked along, Jesus saw a man blind from
birth. His disciples asked him, "Rabbi, who sinned,
this man or his parents, that he was born blind?" Jesus
answered, "Neither this man nor his parents sinned; he
was born blind so that God's works might be revealed
in him. We must work the works of him who sent me
while it is day; night is coming when no one can work.
As long as I am in the world, I am the light of the
world." When he had said this, he spat on the ground
and made mud with the saliva and spread the mud
on the man's eyes, saying to him, "Go, wash in the
pool of Siloam" (which means sent). Then he went and
washed and came back able to see. The neighbors and
those who had seen him before as a beggar began to
ask, "Is this not the man who used to sit and beg?"
Some were saying, "It is he." Others were saying, "No,
but it is someone like him." He kept saying, "I am the
man." But they kept asking him, "Then how were your
eyes opened?" He answered, "The man called Jesus
made mud, spread it on my eyes, and said to me, 'Go
to Siloam and wash.' Then I went and washed and

received my sight." They said to him, "Where is he?"
He said, "I do not know."

Notice what you think and feel as you read the Gospel.

It's all about judging sinners. Jesus' disciples ask
whether a blind man is blind because he is a sinner.
Jesus says no. The blind man, after he receives his
sight, is challenged by those who know him. The Pharisees wonder how a sinner (they mean Jesus) can heal
someone. Jesus says that they are truly the blind ones.

Pray as you are led for yourself and others.

"You are the light of the world, Lord. Be my light. I
want your light to shine upon all who sit in darkness.
I pray for . . ." (Continue in your own words.)

Listen to Jesus.

*My child, do not find fault in others. In judging them, you
err. Only I know the heart.* What else is Jesus saying to
you?

Ask God to show you how to live today.

"I have and do make judgments about others. Shine
your light on me and show me how to undo my judgments. Amen."

Tuesday, March 8, 2016

Know that God is present with you and ready to converse.

"Jesus is aware of my needs. I will wait for him now."

Read the Gospel: John 5:1–16* (2–16).

Now in Jerusalem by the Sheep Gate there is a pool, called in Hebrew Beth-zatha, which has five porticoes. In these lay many invalids—blind, lame, and paralyzed. One man was there who had been ill for thirty-eight years. When Jesus saw him lying there and knew that he had been there a long time, he said to him, "Do you want to be made well?" The sick man answered him, "Sir, I have no one to put me into the pool when the water is stirred up; and while I am making my way, someone else steps down ahead of me." Jesus said to him, "Stand up, take your mat, and walk." At once the man was made well, and he took up his mat, and began to walk.

Now that day was a Sabbath. So the Jews said to the man who had been cured, "It is the Sabbath; it is not lawful for you to carry your mat." But he answered them, "The man who made me well said to me, 'Take up your mat and walk.'" They asked him, "Who is the man who said to you, 'Take it up and walk'?" Now the man who had been healed did not know who it was, for Jesus had disappeared in the crowd that was there. Later Jesus found him in the Temple and said to him,

"See, you have been made well! Do not sin anymore, so that nothing worse happens to you." The man went away and told the Jews that it was Jesus who had made him well. Therefore the Jews started persecuting Jesus, because he was doing such things on the Sabbath.

Notice what you think and feel as you read the Gospel.

The Pharisees always seem concerned about Jesus healing on the Sabbath. Jesus heals the man who had been ill for thirty-eight years.

Pray as you are led for yourself and others.

"Lord, I offer myself in your work of helping others. Let me work alongside you. Jesus . . ." (Continue in your own words.)

Listen to Jesus.

We are working together, my beloved disciple. Do not be discouraged by the difficulties of this world, but live and work in my hope. What else is Jesus saying to you?

Ask God to show you how to live today.

"I will rely on you, Lord, to show me how to live today. Amen."

Wednesday, March 9, 2016

Know that God is present with you and ready to converse.

"Father almighty, you are working in me; Jesus, you are working, too. Let me respond to your Word."

Read the Gospel: John 5:17–30* (17–24).

But Jesus answered them, "My Father is still working, and I also am working." For this reason the Jews were seeking all the more to kill him, because he was not only breaking the Sabbath, but was also calling God his own Father, thereby making himself equal to God.

Jesus said to them, "Very truly, I tell you, the Son can do nothing on his own, but only what he sees the Father doing; for whatever the Father does, the Son does likewise. The Father loves the Son and shows him all that he himself is doing; and he will show him greater works than these, so that you will be astonished. Indeed, just as the Father raises the dead and gives them life, so also the Son gives life to whomever he wishes. The Father judges no one but has given all judgment to the Son, so that all may honor the Son just as they honor the Father. Anyone who does not honor the Son does not honor the Father who sent him. Very truly, I tell you, anyone who hears my word and believes him who sent me has eternal life, and does not come under judgment, but has passed from death to life."

Notice what you think and feel as you read the Gospel.

Jesus affirms that his Father works all the time, and so does he, even on the Sabbath. Like his Father, he gives life to whomever he wishes—even eternal life. The one who believes has already passed from death to life.

Pray as you are led for yourself and others.

"Jesus, you promise resurrection. Your Father has given you all judgment, all authority, all power. I believe in you and your wonderful words of life. I worship you . . ." (Continue in your own words.)

Listen to Jesus.

As my Father loves me, I love you, dear friend. Start here, and reach out to others. What else is Jesus saying to you?

Ask God to show you how to live today.

"I am willing, Lord. I want to do your will as you did the will of your Father. Help me to see it and do it. Amen."

Thursday, March 10, 2016

Know that God is present with you and ready to converse.

"In your presence, Lord, grant me quietness of heart, peace, and joy. I will hear you."

Read the Gospel: John 5:31–47* (33–40, 45–47).

Jesus said, "You sent messengers to John, and he testified to the truth. Not that I accept such human testimony, but I say these things so that you may be saved. He was a burning and shining lamp, and you were willing to rejoice for a while in his light. But I have a testimony greater than John's. The works that the Father has given me to complete, the very works that I am doing, testify on my behalf that the Father has sent me. And the Father who sent me has himself testified on my behalf. You have never heard his voice or seen his form, and you do not have his word abiding in you, because you do not believe him whom he has sent.

"You search the scriptures because you think that in them you have eternal life; and it is they that testify on my behalf. Yet you refuse to come to me to have life. . . . Do not think that I will accuse you before the Father; your accuser is Moses, on whom you have set your hope. If you believed Moses, you would believe me, for he wrote about me. But if you do not believe what he wrote, how will you believe what I say?"

Notice what you think and feel as you read the Gospel.

Jesus challenges the Pharisees and me: How can people believe in Jesus as the Christ when they seek to receive glory from one another and do not seek the glory that comes from God?

Pray as you are led for yourself and others.

"I have enjoyed approval from others, Lord, and I have even been resentful when I didn't get credit I thought I deserved. Let me put all that behind me and seek only you, your approval, your glory . . ." (Continue in your own words.)

Listen to Jesus.

Be generous, honest, and just in your approval of others, especially as you are in authority. You can encourage others by this. Know, too, that people need to do things for their own reasons—and for mine. What else is Jesus saying to you?

Ask God to show you how to live today.

"Lord, give me wisdom to do your will in my relation-ships. Amen."

Friday, March 11, 2016

Know that God is present with you and ready to converse.

"Speak to me, Jesus, for you come from God; you are God's holy Word of truth."

Read the Gospel: John 7:1–2, 10, 25–30* (1–2, 25–30).

After this Jesus went about in Galilee. He did not wish to go about in Judea because the Jews were looking for an opportunity to kill him. Now the Jewish festival of Booths was near. . . .

Now some of the people of Jerusalem were saying, "Is not this the man whom they are trying to kill? And here he is, speaking openly, but they say nothing to him! Can it be that the authorities really know that this is the Messiah? Yet we know where this man is from; but when the Messiah comes, no one will know where he is from." Then Jesus cried out as he was teaching in the Temple, "You know me, and you know where I am from. I have not come on my own. But the one who sent me is true, and you do not know him. I know him, because I am from him, and he sent me." Then they tried to arrest him, but no one laid hands on him, because his hour had not yet come.

Notice what you think and feel as you read the Gospel.

Jesus is brave. He speaks the truth boldly, knowing the hearts of those in Jerusalem who want to arrest him. He tells them they do not know the One who sent him.

Pray as you are led for yourself and others.

"Jesus, I am not brave. I need to be a brave person, doing what's right every day, speaking your truth with all humility . . ." (Continue in your own words.)

Listen to Jesus.

I send my Spirit to strengthen you, to give you the words of truth, to give you what you need to touch hearts with love. What else is Jesus saying to you?

Ask God to show you how to live today.

"Lord, thank you. Show me how to allow my weakness to be your strength today. Amen."

Saturday, March 12, 2016

Know that God is present with you and ready to converse.

"You are patient with me, Lord, as I listen to your Word. I long to grow closer to you."

Read the Gospel: John 7:40–53* (40–49).

When they heard Jesus' words, some in the crowd said, "This is really the prophet." Others said, "This is the Messiah." But some asked, "Surely the Messiah does not come from Galilee, does he? Has not the scripture said that the Messiah is descended from David and comes from Bethlehem, the village where David lived?" So there was a division in the crowd because of him. Some of them wanted to arrest him, but no one laid hands on him.

Then the Temple police went back to the chief priests and Pharisees, who asked them, "Why did you not arrest him?" The police answered, "Never has anyone spoken like this!" Then the Pharisees replied, "Surely you have not been deceived too, have you? Has any one of the authorities or of the Pharisees believed in him? But this crowd, which does not know the law—they are accursed."

Notice what you think and feel as you read the Gospel.

There is considerable confusion among the Jews about the identity of Jesus. Some point out the Messiah is prophesized to come from Bethlehem, not Galilee. When the Temple police go to arrest Jesus, they return without him, saying, "Never has anyone spoken like this!" How fortunate were those who heard Jesus speak!

Pray as you are led for yourself and others.

"Lord, let me hear your voice, full of love, power, and authority. Then help me to return your love and obey you . . ." (Continue in your own words.)

Listen to Jesus.

I know you, dear one. I know what you need. I am the one you need. Ours is a journey of lovers. What else is Jesus saying to you?

Ask God to show you how to live today.

"God, I seek you in all things. Let me glorify you and trust in your ways. Amen."

FIFTH WEEK OF LENT

The proof of love is in the works. Where love exists, it works great things. But when it ceases to act, it ceases to exist.

Saint Gregory the Great

Sunday, March 13, 2016
Fifth Sunday of Lent

**Know that God is present with
you and ready to converse.**

Jesus reveals to us the mercy of God, for he and the
Father are one. We rejoice in his mercy—forgiving us,
healing us, and helping us to forgive others.

When you are ready to listen to the Lord, invite him
with words such as these: "Jesus, you do not condemn
me. Teach me now by your Word and draw me into
your love."

Read the Gospel: John 8:2–11.

Early in the morning Jesus came again to the Temple.
All the people came to him and he sat down and began
to teach them. The scribes and the Pharisees brought a
woman who had been caught in adultery; and making
her stand before all of them, they said to him, "Teacher,
this woman was caught in the very act of committing
adultery. Now in the law Moses commanded us to
stone such women. Now what do you say?" They said
this to test him, so that they might have some charge to
bring against him. Jesus bent down and wrote with his
finger on the ground. When they kept on questioning
him, he straightened up and said to them, "Let anyone
among you who is without sin be the first to throw a
stone at her." And once again he bent down and wrote
on the ground. When they heard it, they went away,

one by one, beginning with the elders; and Jesus was left alone with the woman standing before him. Jesus straightened up and said to her, "Woman, where are they? Has no one condemned you?" She said, "No one, sir." And Jesus said, "Neither do I condemn you. Go your way, and from now on do not sin again."

Notice what you think and feel as you read the Gospel.

Jesus escapes the entrapment by the Pharisees, and the woman escapes stoning. Jesus' words, "Let anyone among you who is without sin be the first to throw a stone," freezes them in shame. What does Jesus say to the woman now?

Pray as you are led for yourself and others.

"Jesus, there is meaning here for me as a judger and for me as a sinner. Let me take this to heart when I am prone to judge. Let me take this to heart when I am tempted to sin again . . ." (Continue in your own words.)

Listen to Jesus.

I am your constant friend, dear one. I strengthen your spirit and grant you wisdom. What else is Jesus saying to you?

Ask God to show you how to live today.

"Lord, how does this Gospel change me in my dealings with others? In my dealings with you? Amen."

Monday, March 14, 2016

**Know that God is present with
you and ready to converse.**

"Jesus, let your Word raise me up and give me life."

Read the Gospel: John 11:1–45*
(1, 5–6, 17–27, 34–45).

Now a certain man was ill, Lazarus of Bethany, the village of Mary and her sister Martha. . . . Accordingly, though Jesus loved Martha and her sister and Lazarus, after having heard that Lazarus was ill, he stayed two days longer in the place where he was. . . .

When Jesus arrived, he found that Lazarus had already been in the tomb four days. Now Bethany was near Jerusalem, some two miles away, and many of the Jews had come to Martha and Mary to console them about their brother. When Martha heard that Jesus was coming, she went and met him, while Mary stayed at home. Martha said to Jesus, "Lord, if you had been here, my brother would not have died. But even now I know that God will give you whatever you ask of him." Jesus said to her, "Your brother will rise again." Martha said to him, "I know that he will rise again in the resurrection on the last day." Jesus said to her, "I am the resurrection and the life. Those who believe in me, even though they die, will live, and everyone who lives and believes in me will never die. Do you believe this?" She said to him, "Yes, Lord, I believe that you are the Messiah, the Son of God, the one coming into the world." . . .

He said, "Where have you laid him?" They said to him, "Lord, come and see." Jesus began to weep. So the Jews said, "See how he loved him!" But some of them said, "Could not he who opened the eyes of the blind man have kept this man from dying?"

Then Jesus, again greatly disturbed, came to the tomb. It was a cave, and a stone was lying against it. Jesus said, "Take away the stone." Martha, the sister of the dead man, said to him, "Lord, already there is a stench because he has been dead four days." Jesus said to her, "Did I not tell you that if you believed, you would see the glory of God?" So they took away the stone. And Jesus looked upward and said, "Father, I thank you for having heard me. I knew that you always hear me, but I have said this for the sake of the crowd standing here, so that they may believe that you sent me." When he had said this, he cried with a loud voice, "Lazarus, come out!" The dead man came out, his hands and feet bound with strips of cloth, and his face wrapped in a cloth. Jesus said to them, "Unbind him, and let him go."

Many of the Jews therefore, who had come with Mary and had seen what Jesus did, believed in him.

Notice what you think and feel as you read the Gospel.

Jesus did nothing by chance. He proclaims himself to be the resurrection and the life, and he proves it by raising Lazarus, already dead four days. Why does this event move Jesus to tears?

Pray as you are led for yourself and others.

"Jesus, you experienced the loss of family and loved ones. Death may be natural in this life, but it has no place in your kingdom. I praise you, for you give everlasting life to those who believe in you . . ." (Continue in your own words.)

Listen to Jesus.

You see how difficult it is for some to believe. Let me strengthen your faith in me. If you want that, open your heart to me now. What else is Jesus saying to you?

Ask God to show you how to live today.

"Thank you for strengthening me in faith, hope, and love. Make me an instrument of your peace today. Amen."

Tuesday, March 15, 2016

**Know that God is present with
you and ready to converse.**

"Jesus, Son of the Father, I rejoice in your presence. Let
me know you in your Word."

Read the Gospel: John 8:21–30.

Again he said to them, "I am going away, and you
will search for me, but you will die in your sin. Where
I am going, you cannot come." Then the Jews said,
"Is he going to kill himself? Is that what he means by
saying, 'Where I am going, you cannot come'?" He
said to them, "You are from below, I am from above;
you are of this world, I am not of this world. I told you
that you would die in your sins, for you will die in
your sins unless you believe that I am he." They said
to him, "Who are you?" Jesus said to them, "Why do
I speak to you at all? I have much to say about you
and much to condemn; but the one who sent me is
true, and I declare to the world what I have heard from
him." They did not understand that he was speaking to
them about the Father. So Jesus said, "When you have
lifted up the Son of Man, then you will realize that I
am he, and that I do nothing on my own, but I speak
these things as the Father instructed me. And the one
who sent me is with me; he has not left me alone, for I
always do what is pleasing to him." As he was saying
these things, many believed in him.

**Notice what you think and feel
as you read the Gospel.**

Jesus, who always did what was pleasing to his Father,
declares that his message has been the same since the
beginning of his ministry. He now prophesies to the
ones who doubt him that they will know that "I am
he" when they have "lifted up the Son of Man."

Pray as you are led for yourself and others.

"Brave Jesus, you speak of the power of the cross. The
shame of crucifixion you would transform to glory, salvation, and life. Your own would recognize you there
. . ." (Continue in your own words.)

Listen to Jesus.

*I came to the world to reconcile humankind to God. I am
joyful for each one who believes in me and receives my salvation. I am happy in you, dear disciple.* What else is Jesus
saying to you?

Ask God to show you how to live today.

"Jesus, I have many choices today. I begin by choosing
you. Be with me in all my choices. Amen."

Wednesday, March 16, 2016

Know that God is present with you and ready to converse.

"Your words are truth and life, Lord. I turn to you now."

Read the Gospel: John 8:31–42.

Then Jesus said to the Jews who had believed in him, "If you continue in my word, you are truly my disciples; and you will know the truth, and the truth will make you free." They answered him, "We are descendants of Abraham and have never been slaves to anyone. What do you mean by saying, 'You will be made free'?"

Jesus answered them, "Very truly, I tell you, everyone who commits sin is a slave to sin. The slave does not have a permanent place in the household; the son has a place there forever. So if the Son makes you free, you will be free indeed. I know that you are descendants of Abraham; yet you look for an opportunity to kill me, because there is no place in you for my word. I declare what I have seen in the Father's presence; as for you, you should do what you have heard from the Father."

They answered him, "Abraham is our father." Jesus said to them, "If you were Abraham's children, you would be doing what Abraham did, but now you are trying to kill me, a man who has told you the truth that

I heard from God. This is not what Abraham did. You are indeed doing what your father does." They said to him, "We are not illegitimate children; we have one father, God himself." Jesus said to them, "If God were your Father, you would love me, for I came from God and now I am here. I did not come on my own, but he sent me."

Notice what you think and feel as you read the Gospel.

"If you continue in my word," Jesus says, "you are truly my disciples." We will know the truth, and it will make us free. Why do so many not hear him?

Pray as you are led for yourself and others.

"Jesus, I seek to do my part to continue in your word. Teach me the truth, all that you have for me, and make me free to do God's will, as you did . . ." (Continue in your own words.)

Listen to Jesus.

You are right to seek me here in the Gospels and in prayer. I share with you truth that will bless you and bear fruit all your life. What else is Jesus saying to you?

Ask God to show you how to live today.

"Lord, I place my whole self and my whole day into your care. Show me ways I can care for others. Amen."

Thursday, March 17, 2016

Know that God is present with you and ready to converse.

"Eternal Word of the Father, I sit at your feet. I will hear and keep your Word."

Read the Gospel: John 8:51–59.

Jesus said, "Very truly, I tell you, whoever keeps my word will never see death." The Jews said to him, "Now we know that you have a demon. Abraham died, and so did the prophets; yet you say, 'Whoever keeps my word will never taste death.' Are you greater than our father Abraham, who died? The prophets also died. Who do you claim to be?" Jesus answered, "If I glorify myself, my glory is nothing. It is my Father who glorifies me, he of whom you say, 'He is our God,' though you do not know him. But I know him; if I would say that I do not know him, I would be a liar like you. But I do know him and I keep his word. Your ancestor Abraham rejoiced that he would see my day; he saw it and was glad." Then the Jews said to him, "You are not yet fifty years old, and have you seen Abraham?" Jesus said to them, "Very truly, I tell you, before Abraham was, I am." So they picked up stones to throw at him, but Jesus hid himself and went out of the Temple.

Notice what you think and feel as you read the Gospel.

Jesus says that if anyone keeps his word, that one will not taste death. He redefines life. He reveals God. And those who hear him scorn him and want to kill him.

Pray as you are led for yourself and others.

"Jesus, help me to understand, believe, and keep your word, for I want to live forever. I want to be close to God . . ." (Continue in your own words.)

Listen to Jesus.

It is not so difficult, my child. I draw you into my life with love and truth. Where else would you go? What else is Jesus saying to you?

Ask God to show you how to live today.

"I have fears, Jesus, but I have no one but you. Let me walk in your word today, for my good and the good of others. Amen."

Friday, March 18, 2016

Know that God is present with you and ready to converse.

"Lord, you are good to extend your glory to me, even now as I prepare to converse with you."

Read the Gospel: John 10:31–42* (31–39).

The Jews took up stones again to stone him. Jesus replied, "I have shown you many good works from the Father. For which of these are you going to stone me?" The Jews answered, "It is not for a good work that we are going to stone you, but for blasphemy, because you, though only a human being, are making yourself God." Jesus answered, "Is it not written in your law, 'I said, you are gods'? If those to whom the word of God came were called 'gods'—and the scripture cannot be annulled—can you say that the one whom the Father has sanctified and sent into the world is blaspheming because I said, 'I am God's Son'? If I am not doing the works of my Father, then do not believe me. But if I do them, even though you do not believe me, believe the works, so that you may know and understand that the Father is in me and I am in the Father." Then they tried to arrest him again, but he escaped from their hands.

Notice what you think and feel as you read the Gospel.

Jesus continues to assert that he is one with the Father and does the works of his Father. They want to stone him or arrest him, but somehow he slips through their fingers, as he has done before. His time has not yet come. Many come to him and believe in him.

Pray as you are led for yourself and others.

"Jesus, I believe in you. I thank the Father for sending you. Where would the world be without you?" (Continue in your own words.)

Listen to Jesus.

I am the light of the world, but some choose to remain in darkness. Do not judge them, but love them. I give you the power of my love. What else is Jesus saying to you?

Ask God to show you how to live today.

"Sometimes I am frustrated that I cannot do more, dear Jesus. Show me ways that I can reflect your light and your love today. Amen."

Saturday, March 19, 2016
Saint Joseph, husband of Mary

**Know that God is present with
you and ready to converse.**

"Master of the universe, I glorify you. You are with me now. Guide me in your perfect way."

**Read the Gospel: Matthew 1:16,
18–21, 24a* (18–21, 24a)**

Now the birth of Jesus the Messiah took place in this way. When his mother Mary had been engaged to Joseph, but before they lived together, she was found to be with child from the Holy Spirit. Her husband, Joseph, being a righteous man and unwilling to expose her to public disgrace, planned to dismiss her quietly. But just when he had resolved to do this, an angel of the Lord appeared to him in a dream and said, "Joseph, son of David, do not be afraid to take Mary as your wife, for the child conceived in her is from the Holy Spirit. She will bear a son, and you are to name him Jesus, for he will save his people from their sins." . . .

When Joseph awoke from sleep, he did as the angel of the Lord commanded him.

Notice what you think and feel as you read the Gospel.

Joseph receives the message from the angel and changes his plans. He stays with Mary and waits for the birth of Jesus, the Savior of the world.

Pray as you are led for yourself and others.

"Joseph, you are a just and wise man. You obeyed God. Let me do as you did. Pray for me . . ." (Continue in your own words.)

Listen to Jesus.

We honor Joseph, friend, because he did the will of God. To be like him, surrender yourself to the will of God. I will show you how. What else is Jesus saying to you?

Ask God to show you how to live today.

"Give me wisdom, Lord. Give me power to act simply and decisively in doing the will of God today and every day of my life. Amen."

HOLY WEEK

The life of faith is a journey. . . . Journeying is an art, because if we're always in a hurry, we get tired and don't arrive at our journey's goal. If we stop, we don't go forward and we also miss the goal. Journeying is precisely the art of looking toward the horizon, thinking where we want to go but also enduring the fatigue of the journey. . . . Walking in community, with friends, with those who love us—that helps us. It helps us to arrive precisely at that goal, that 'there' where we're supposed to arrive.

Pope Francis

Sunday, March 20, 2016
Palm Sunday

**Know that God is present with
you and ready to converse.**

When Jesus entered Jerusalem for the last time, he rode
on a borrowed colt, and he humbled himself to receive
honor from the people. The people welcoming him did
not know that he had come to suffer and die there, but
Jesus knew.

When you are ready, begin by joining the crowds
praising Jesus: "Blessed is the King who comes in the
name of the Lord. Glory in the highest."

Read the Gospel: Luke 19:28–40.

After he had said this, he went on ahead, going up to
Jerusalem.

When he had come near Bethphage and Bethany,
at the place called the Mount of Olives, he sent two
of the disciples, saying, "Go into the village ahead of
you, and as you enter it you will find tied there a colt
that has never been ridden. Untie it and bring it here.
If anyone asks you, 'Why are you untying it?' just
say this: 'The Lord needs it.'" So those who were sent
departed and found it as he had told them. As they
were untying the colt, its owners asked them, "Why
are you untying the colt?" They said, "The Lord needs
it." Then they brought it to Jesus; and after throwing
their cloaks on the colt, they set Jesus on it. As he rode

along, people kept spreading their cloaks on the road. As he was now approaching the path down from the Mount of Olives, the whole multitude of the disciples began to praise God joyfully with a loud voice for all the deeds of power that they had seen, saying,

"Blessed is the king
who comes in the name of the Lord!
Peace in heaven,
and glory in the highest heaven!"

Some of the Pharisees in the crowd said to him, "Teacher, order your disciples to stop." He answered, "I tell you, if these were silent, the stones would shout out."

Notice what you think and feel as you read the Gospel.

The Lord enters Jerusalem for the last time on a borrowed colt. The multitudes rejoice and sing his praises. When the Pharisees object to it, Jesus tells them that the stones would shout out praise if the people were silent. He knows who he is—God in the flesh.

Pray as you are led for yourself and others.

"Let me praise you, too, good Savior, as you head in ironic triumph toward your passion and death in Jerusalem . . ." (Continue in your own words.)

Listen to Jesus.

I did it all out of love for the multitudes, and for love for you, child. I did not seek praise or blame in this world, but I sought only to do my Father's will. What else is Jesus saying to you?

Ask God to show you how to live today.

"How may I learn from you today, Lord? How may I follow you? Amen."

Monday, March 21, 2016

Know that God is present with you and ready to converse.

"Spirit of the Lord, you were present with Jesus, and you are present with Jesus now. Thank you for your presence with me as I read God's Word."

Read the Gospel: Luke 4:16–21.

When Jesus came to Nazareth, where he had been brought up, he went to the synagogue on the Sabbath day, as was his custom. He stood up to read, and the scroll of the prophet Isaiah was given to him. He unrolled the scroll and found the place where it was written:

"The Spirit of the Lord is upon me,
        because he has anointed me
            to bring good news to the poor.

He has sent me to proclaim release to the captives
and recovery of sight to the blind,
to let the oppressed go free,
to proclaim the year of the Lord's favor."

And he rolled up the scroll, gave it back to the attendant, and sat down. The eyes of all in the synagogue were fixed on him. Then he began to say to them, "Today this scripture has been fulfilled in your hearing."

Notice what you think and feel as you read the Gospel.

Jesus begins his ministry in his home synagogue reading a great messianic passage from Isaiah. Clearly, his identity as the Christ was clear to him at the beginning; it did not evolve. He is the one who fulfills all the messianic prophesies of Isaiah (and all the prophets). Yet these are the people of his hometown who know him and his parents. What do they think?

Pray as you are led for yourself and others.

"Lord, I sometimes lack understanding of your Word and your ways. Let the Spirit enlighten me that I may serve you better . . ." (Continue in your own words.)

Listen to Jesus.

Practice patience, my child. Quiet yourself before me. I have things to tell you that I want you to know. What else is Jesus saying to you?

Ask God to show you how to live today.

"Thank you for your consoling words, Lord. Let me stay with you and learn from you all day. Amen."

Tuesday, March 22, 2016

Know that God is present with you and ready to converse.

"When I seek you, Lord, you are already found. You work in my heart."

Read the Gospel: John 13:21–33, 36–38* (21–33).

After saying this Jesus was troubled in spirit, and declared, "Very truly, I tell you, one of you will betray me." The disciples looked at one another, uncertain of whom he was speaking. One of his disciples—the one whom Jesus loved—was reclining next to him; Simon Peter therefore motioned to him to ask Jesus of whom he was speaking. So while reclining next to Jesus, he asked him, "Lord, who is it?" Jesus answered, "It is the one to whom I give this piece of bread when I have dipped it in the dish." So when he had dipped the piece of bread, he gave it to Judas son of Simon Iscariot. After he received the piece of bread, Satan entered into him. Jesus said to him, "Do quickly what you are going to do." Now no one at the table knew why he said this to him. Some thought that, because Judas had the common purse, Jesus was telling him,

"Buy what we need for the festival"; or that he should give something to the poor. So, after receiving the piece of bread, he immediately went out. And it was night.

When he had gone out, Jesus said, "Now the Son of Man has been glorified, and God has been glorified in him. If God has been glorified in him, God will also glorify him in himself and will glorify him at once. Little children, I am with you only a little longer. You will look for me, and as I said to the Jews so now I say to you, 'Where I am going, you cannot come.'"

Notice what you think and feel as you read the Gospel.

When John lies close to the heart of Jesus, the Lord speaks to him secretly about his betrayal by Judas. The other disciples misunderstand. Jesus looks forward to his crucifixion as his glorification.

Pray as you are led for yourself and others.

"I want to be your beloved disciple, lie close to your heart, and hear your secret words just for me. Lord, let me follow you even to death and never deny you . . ." (Continue in your own words.)

Listen to Jesus.

You are my beloved disciple, and I speak to you in secret. Do not be afraid of what is coming. Stay here with me. I will tell you what to do. What else is Jesus saying to you?

Ask God to show you how to live today.

"I resolve to stay close to you, gentle Savior. For how else can I keep your commandments to love God and others with all my heart? Amen."

Wednesday, March 23, 2016

Know that God is present with you and ready to converse.

"You spent that last Passover with your friends, even the one who would betray you. Spend time with me now, Jesus, and teach me by your Word."

Read the Gospel: Matthew 26:14–25.

Then one of the Twelve, who was called Judas Iscariot, went to the chief priests and said, "What will you give me if I betray him to you?" They paid him thirty pieces of silver. And from that moment he began to look for an opportunity to betray him.

On the first day of Unleavened Bread the disciples came to Jesus, saying, "Where do you want us to make the preparations for you to eat the Passover?" He said, "Go into the city to a certain man, and say to him, 'The Teacher says, my time is near; I will keep the Passover at your house with my disciples.'" So the disciples did as Jesus had directed them, and they prepared the Passover meal.

When it was evening, he took his place with the Twelve; and while they were eating, he said, "Truly I tell you, one of you will betray me." And they became greatly distressed and began to say to him one after another, "Surely not I, Lord?" He answered, "The one who has dipped his hand into the bowl with me will betray me. The Son of Man goes as it is written of him, but woe to that one by whom the Son of Man is betrayed! It would have been better for that one not to have been born." Judas, who betrayed him, said, "Surely not I, Rabbi?" He replied, "You have said so."

Notice what you think and feel as you read the Gospel.

Was Judas motivated by thirty pieces of silver? Was he pretending to believe in Jesus all along? Was Jesus able to get through to him? Judas acted by his own choice.

Pray as you are led for yourself and others.

"There are mysteries in your Word, Lord. There are mysteries in my life. Evil is a mystery. But I choose good. I choose you . . ." (Continue in your own words.)

Listen to Jesus.

Pray for those who do evil. All things are possible with God, even the salvation of sinners. What else is Jesus saying to you?

Ask God to show you how to live today.

"Dear Lord and Savior, I need you all day long, your love and your wisdom. Thank you. Amen."

Thursday, March 24, 2016
Holy Thursday

**Know that God is present with
you and ready to converse.**

"Teacher and Lord, I am ready to learn from you
today."

Read the Gospel: John 13:1–15.

Now before the festival of the Passover, Jesus knew
that his hour had come to depart from this world and
go to the Father. Having loved his own who were in the
world, he loved them to the end. The devil had already
put it into the heart of Judas son of Simon Iscariot to
betray him. And during supper Jesus, knowing that
the Father had given all things into his hands, and that
he had come from God and was going to God, got up
from the table, took off his outer robe, and tied a towel
around himself. Then he poured water into a basin and
began to wash the disciples' feet and to wipe them
with the towel that was tied around him. He came to
Simon Peter, who said to him, "Lord, are you going
to wash my feet?" Jesus answered, "You do not know
now what I am doing, but later you will understand."
Peter said to him, "You will never wash my feet." Jesus
answered, "Unless I wash you, you have no share with
me." Simon Peter said to him, "Lord, not my feet only
but also my hands and my head!" Jesus said to him,
"One who has bathed does not need to wash, except

for the feet, but is entirely clean. And you are clean, though not all of you." For he knew who was to betray him; for this reason he said, "Not all of you are clean."

After he had washed their feet, had put on his robe, and had returned to the table, he said to them, "Do you know what I have done to you? You call me Teacher and Lord—and you are right, for that is what I am. So if I, your Lord and Teacher, have washed your feet, you also ought to wash one another's feet. For I have set you an example, that you also should do as I have done to you."

Notice what you think and feel as you read the Gospel.

Facing a horrible death, Jesus thinks about his friends and gives them a great life lesson in humble service of others. Jesus' love and goodness overwhelms me.

Pray as you are led for yourself and others.

"Wash me, Lord, so that I may be clean, and let me also serve others—friends and enemies—that I may be like you, my Teacher and Lord . . ." (Continue in your own words.)

Listen to Jesus.

You understand me, dear student. I love to show you myself. I would love you to do the works that I do. What else is Jesus saying to you?

Ask God to show you how to live today.

"Jesus, it would give me great pleasure to do your works and to do them as you would have me do them. Show your simple child what to do to be like you. Amen."

Friday, March 25, 2016
Good Friday

**Know that God is present with
you and ready to converse.**

"May I console Jesus during his passion and death? Father, let me be present with him and hear his voice."

Read the Gospel: John 18:1–19:42* (19:17–30).

So they took Jesus; and carrying the cross by himself, he went out to what is called the Place of the Skull, which in Hebrew is called Golgotha. There they cruci-fied him, and with him two others, one on either side, with Jesus between them. Pilate also had an inscription written and put on the cross. It read, "Jesus of Naza-reth, the King of the Jews." Many of the Jews read this inscription, because the place where Jesus was cruci-fied was near the city; and it was written in Hebrew, in Latin, and in Greek. Then the chief priests of the Jews said to Pilate, "Do not write, 'The King of the Jews,' but, 'This man said, I am King of the Jews.'" Pilate answered, "What I have written I have written." When the soldiers had crucified Jesus, they took his clothes and divided them into four parts, one for each soldier. They also took his tunic; now the tunic was seamless, woven in one piece from the top. So they said to one another, "Let us not tear it, but cast lots for it to see who will get it." This was to fulfill what the scripture says,

"They divided my clothes among themselves,
and for my clothing they cast lots."

And that is what the soldiers did.

Meanwhile, standing near the cross of Jesus were his mother, and his mother's sister, Mary the wife of Clopas, and Mary Magdalene. When Jesus saw his mother and the disciple whom he loved standing beside her, he said to his mother, "Woman, here is your son." Then he said to the disciple, "Here is your mother." And from that hour the disciple took her into his own home.

After this, when Jesus knew that all was now finished, he said (in order to fulfill the scripture), "I am thirsty." A jar full of sour wine was standing there. So they put a sponge full of the wine on a branch of hyssop and held it to his mouth. When Jesus had received the wine, he said, "It is finished." Then he bowed his head and gave up his spirit.

Notice what you think and feel as you read the Gospel.

This is the narrative of your passion, Jesus. I empathize with every painful detail, and I love you for taking on the sins of the world. You say to Pilate, "Everyone who is of the truth hears my voice."

Pray as you are led for yourself and others.

"I need to hear your voice, Jesus. May your words in this Gospel give me courage and wisdom when I, too, have a cross to carry or suffering to bear. Lamb of God, have mercy on me . . ." (Continue in your own words.)

Listen to Jesus.

You do console me, beloved disciple. Do you know that I would have gone to my death for you alone? Follow me. What else is Jesus saying to you?

Ask God to show you how to live today.

"The great saints follow you, Lord. I am just myself. Please take me by the hand and help me to do your will. Amen."

Saturday, March 26, 2016
Easter Vigil

Know that God is present with you and ready to converse.

"Rise up in victory, strong Son of God. Let me attend to your Word."

Read the Gospel: Luke 24:1–12.

But on the first day of the week, at early dawn, the women came to the tomb, taking the spices that they had prepared. They found the stone rolled away from the tomb, but when they went in, they did not find the body. While they were perplexed about this, suddenly two men in dazzling clothes stood beside them. The women were terrified and bowed their faces to the ground, but the men said to them, "Why do you look for the living among the dead? He is not here, but has risen. Remember how he told you, while he was still in Galilee, that the Son of Man must be handed over to sinners, and be crucified, and on the third day rise again." Then they remembered his words, and returning from the tomb, they told all this to the eleven and to all the rest. Now it was Mary Magdalene, Joanna, Mary the mother of James, and the other women with them who told this to the apostles. But these words seemed to them an idle tale, and they did not believe them. But Peter got up and ran to the tomb; stooping and looking in, he saw the linen cloths by themselves; then he went home, amazed at what had happened.

Notice what you think and feel as you read the Gospel.

The eleven do not believe the report of the three women after they find the tomb empty and hear the explanation of the two angels. Peter runs to the tomb and confirms that it is empty, and he goes home wondering.

Pray as you are led for yourself and others.

"Jesus, I know the rest of the story, which Peter cannot know. He wonders what this could mean. You would reveal the Resurrection to him later. Reveal it also to me, so I can share in your victory . . ." (Continue in your own words.)

Listen to Jesus.

This was my work, my sign, my glory, that I would take on the sins of the whole world, be put to death, and rise again. Now God is near to all. My kingdom is forever. Whoever will, let him or her come to me. What else is Jesus saying to you?

Ask God to show you how to live today.

"I glorify you, Lord, along with the billions of your redeemed throughout the ages. Stay with us, Lord, to the end. I thank you. Give me gratitude in true recognition of your glory. Amen."

Sunday, March 27, 2016
Easter Sunday

**Know that God is present with
you and ready to converse.**

After Jesus' brutal execution and burial, the disciples
discover the empty tomb. They are slow to believe. We
recognize the weakness of our own faith, but we know,
too, that faith comes by hearing the Word of God.

When you are ready, invite Jesus to reveal himself
to you by his Word: "Alleluia. You are risen from the
dead. Come into my heart, Lord. Come into my life."

Read the Gospel: John 20:1–9.

Early on the first day of the week, while it was still
dark, Mary Magdalene came to the tomb and saw that
the stone had been removed from the tomb. So she ran
and went to Simon Peter and the other disciple, the
one whom Jesus loved, and said to them, "They have
taken the Lord out of the tomb, and we do not know
where they have laid him." Then Peter and the other
disciple set out and went toward the tomb. The two
were running together, but the other disciple outran
Peter and reached the tomb first. He bent down to look
in and saw the linen wrappings lying there, but he did
not go in. Then Simon Peter came, following him, and
went into the tomb. He saw the linen wrappings lying
there, and the cloth that had been on Jesus' head, not
lying with the linen wrappings but rolled up in a place

by itself. Then the other disciple, who reached the tomb first, also went in, and he saw and believed; for as yet they did not understand the scripture, that he must rise from the dead.

Notice what you think and feel as you read the Gospel.

Finally the disciples Peter and John see the empty tomb. What did they believe? How could anyone take in the fact of Jesus being raised from the dead?

Pray as you are led for yourself and others.

"Lord, I, too, can be slow to faith. Your resurrection was the most amazing event of all time. I pray for those who doubt your resurrection. Let them see the truth . . ." (Continue in your own words.)

Listen to Jesus.

I have shown the power of God to all people, though some choose not to believe it. You do. You are my beloved disciple. I welcome you into my kingdom of life, love, peace, and joy forever. What else is Jesus saying to you?

Ask God to show you how to live today.

"Lord, you do so much for me. How may I serve others in the same spirit, today, tomorrow, and for my whole life? Amen."

Please Take Our Survey!

Now that you've finished reading *Sacred Reading for Lent 2016*, please go to **avemariapress.com/feedback** to take a brief survey about your experience. Ave Maria Press and the Apostleship of Prayer appreciate your feedback.

The Apostleship of Prayer is an international Jesuit prayer ministry that reaches more than fifty million members worldwide through its popular website, *ApostleshipofPrayer.org*, and through talks, conferences, publications, and retreats such as Hearts on Fire. Known as "the pope's prayer group," the Apostleship's mission is to encourage Christians to make a daily offering of themselves to the Lord and at whose center is the love of the Sacred Heart of Jesus. Douglas Leonard has served as executive director of the Apostleship of Prayer in the United States since 2006.

The
SACRED
READING
Series

Inspired by the traditions of Ignatian spirituality, the Sacred Reading series by the Apostleship of Prayer—an international Jesuit prayer ministry—is a unique guide to the use of lectio divinia through a simple, six-step process that provides a prayerful and imaginative exploration of the daily gospel readings and helps readers look for application in their own lives.

Ignatian Spirituality for Every Season

Find next year's editions wherever books and eBooks are sold.
For more information, **visit avemariapress.com.**

AVE MARIA PRESS
A Ministry of the United States
Province of Holy Cross